A FRANK TALK ON

THE M WORD

Is It Really a Sin?

BY FRANK FRIEDMANN

ISBN 978-1974205912

Previously published under the title:
Masturbation, What Does God Really Think?

Published by Lazarus Media Productions

www.lazarusmediaproductions.com

CONTENTS

FOREWORD

I first met Frank Friedmann in the early 90s when I arrogantly walked into his counseling office with my fiancée Kym, ready to upstage him with my incredible knowledge of the Bible and vast amount of scripture memorization. Because I had experienced long nights of traveling on the road in professional baseball, I had memorized a few books of the New Testament in their entirety (and I was very proud of it!). But after an hour or so with Frank, I humbly walked out of his office wondering if I really understood anything I had committed to memory at all. Pulling from scripture, Frank had walked me through the purpose of the Ten Commandments and put the grace of God in my hands, in a person named Jesus. Mix in some revelation from the Holy Spirit and I began to experience a relationship with God and a FREEDOM from guilt and the need to perform I had longed for my whole life. I was thankful.

If it's true that lies lead to bondage and the truth sets us free, then it's imperative that we know and understand the truth when it comes to major issues in the body of Christ. Especially issues we like to avoid. Masturbation is one of those issues. One of my friends is a psychiatrist. He recently lectured at a highly touted conference for many of our nation's pastors and spiritual leaders. He led off with the question, "How many of you as fathers speak to your teenagers about masturbation?" Not one person raised their hand. I was sad to know that the shame and guilt over masturbation, an issue that once caused a classmate of mine to take his own life, was not even addressed by some of our nation's top Christian leaders in their own families. I also wondered, if they did speak to them, what would they say?

In a politically correct world that warns us if we want to keep our friends we shouldn't talk about money, sex, religion, or politics, Frank Friedmann shatters boundaries and takes a huge risk with this book by tackling this hush-hush subject matter almost everyone avoids. And most importantly, he goes straight to the heart of the matter, teaching straight from the scriptures. This book offers freedom from popular theories of what "sexual sin" truly is and what it is not.

Make NO mistake, this book is DESPERATELY NEEDED in our culture today for not only for youth but for grown men and women as well. Like Frank, I am asking you take a risk, be a forward thinker, and buy this book without a brown paper bag. The issue of masturbation does not have to be taboo any longer. It is vital that we let God's Word permeate our hearts and speak to us on all topics not just the ones that make us comfortable. It's time to be free.

Paul Byrd (Major League Baseball All-Star, Fox Sports Emmy Nominated Broadcaster, and author of best-selling book *Free Byrd*)

PREFACE

"You're writing a book on what?"

"MASTURBATION?"

"Why would you write a book on *that*?"

As I shared this latest writing project with people, this was by far the most common response I received. If people didn't outright say it they certainly expressed the opinion visibly with the quizzical looks on their faces. Why would one write a book on such a topic?

And, in all honesty, that's a fair question. The answer is quite simple. We as a church need clear, Biblical teaching on masturbation. As a topic, it's largely avoided and associated with shame. The responses I just shared with you underscore that truth.

The Bible calls us to come and reason together around the truth of what God has Himself taught in His Word. And where the Bible does not explain to us explicitly what He says about a particular issue, we are to take what He has said in principle, and function, as iron sharpening iron, to hone our appropriation of those principles in a way that dynamically affects the way we live.

Yet sadly, through ignorance, fear, propriety, and perhaps prudishness, we have left instruction on such issues to chance individual discovery. Even worse, through the Church's silence we have allowed the world's philosophy and ways to shape our thinking and our behavior. It is time for that approach on this topic to come to an end! It is time for us to be courageous! It is time for us to love each other enough to come together and hammer out this issue in accordance with what the Bible does teach us and come at this issue armed with truth in our hearts!

To that end, I offer you this study. I encourage you to not only read this book, but also to go to the book of all books—the Bible—and test what you read here. See if it harmonizes with what you find in Father's Word. My heart for this book is that people will discover the truth that sets men free as they rely on the Spirit of God to guide them.

INTRODUCTION

As a Pastor and counselor, I can attest that masturbation tends to be a very "touchy" subject and may "rub" some people the wrong way (both puns intended).

With this in mind, I ask one thing: please read this little book in its entirety. Read with a sense of humor and, more importantly, read with an open heart and prayerful spirit. Masturbation has been the subject of a lot of conjecture in the church—conjecture that has directly placed guilt and shame on God's children. My friend, we have an enemy that ministers enough of those commodities without our conjecture adding to his onslaught against us. We need to make sure that what we are saying on any given subject is what God himself has taught on that subject. Once we have determined what God says, we must take care to speak what God speaks in the same manner in which He speaks it. As the Apostle Paul stated, we are to speak the truth in love.

In this short book, it is my hope that we will clear up a lot of the confusion surrounding this topic. My goal is to enable you to walk in freedom! That's why we're here, isn't it? We want to know what the truth is! Jesus said it beautifully: when we come to know the truth, the truth will set us free!

Father, there is so much confusion and error on this subject, and it is causing no small amount of struggle in the lives of your people. As we search out your Word, may your Spirit guide us into all truth and protect us from any error. It is time for truth to reign in this arena and we are trusting you to bring us to your truth. Thank you, Father, in Jesus' name. Amen!

WHY TALK ABOUT MASTURBATION?

Now when it comes to masturbation, I want to be careful with my words. First and foremost, as I said earlier in jest, I now say in all seriousness: it is a touchy subject. People are afraid to talk about it and very often get very uncomfortable when it is discussed. Further, a frank and truthful discussion is necessary because so many, many people struggle with this issue.

If the church doesn't address the issue of masturbation, where will people look for wisdom and answers? Google, probably, right? (By the way, I don't recommend that method...) The fact of the matter is that since we possess Father's Word, the body of Christ is the forum where such tough topics like masturbation need to be addressed.

Sadly, the following cartoon is a pretty decent portrayal of what happens inside the church whenever this issue comes up. The church tends to treat this

Illustration by Christine Leone

Taking attendance was usually the most difficult part of the night.

issue—in fact, 'treat the issue' is probably the wrong choice of words—the church very often, *does not* treat the issue. That my friends, is a tragedy!

The church's treatment of this subject has typically resulted in misinformation and condemnation. You know what I'm referring to, right? "If you masturbate, you'll go blind" or, "If you masturbate, you'll grow warts on your hands!", and the like. That kind of misinformation is no longer as prevalent in our modern culture, but the confusion and the guilt surrounding this issue abounds.

Another misconception is that masturbation is only a male issue. Perhaps you have heard the joke that there are only two kinds of men: those who have masturbated, and those who lie. Though there may be some truth to that statement, I've found through my years of experience that masturbation is not only a masculine issue. Many women who have passed through our counseling office have confirmed this.

The issue of masturbation is laden with guilt and condemnation. As a speaker and counselor, I get phone calls and letters from a wide variety of people all over the country. Recently, a fellow from out of state emailed me. He wrote that since I was out of state, he felt like I was someone who was 'safe' to talk to. He shared with me that masturbation was the supreme struggle in his life and that he was riddled with guilt and shame because of it. It was quite obvious in talking with him that he believed he was the only one with such a struggle. Feeling isolated and alone is one of the nasty by-products of our failure to deal with this issue openly. When we believe we are the only one who struggles with such an issue, we are easy prey for the enemy to discourage us in our walk with God.

On another occasion, I was talking with a young college student and he shared with me how his Bible study handled this issue. They decided to form an accountability group to "keep each other accountable" to not masturbate. Each week when they gathered together, they would take turns and report to the others how successful they were at avoiding the "sin of masturbation". The agreement between them was that if one of them masturbated, they had to put a dollar into the group jar, one for each time they had done it. I said to the young man, "How did that work?" And he said, "Well basically, we all lied."

This is the typical fashion in which the church tends to deal with this issue. Since so many people in the church believe masturbation is a sin, we have to make every effort and take every step available to us to stop this behavior. If we can't stop it, we will hide and often lie to each other to do so. Personally, I am not a big fan of accountability groups or even accountability partners. I mean, just think about the word... ACCOUNTABILITY! I don't know about you, but for me that conjures up images of a strict finger pointed sternly, right at my nose! Rather than producing an environment of acceptance in which I might sheepishly venture forth with some semblance of honesty, that word makes me shrink back in fear. I would much rather proclaim the need for "encouragement" groups that minister acceptance and love in the midst of pursuing the truth. I believe this is the great need for the body of Christ in every behavioral arena that might bring us into guilt and shame. Of course, the greatest need is to arrive at the truth of what God Himself says concerning this issue. Sadly my friends, we have very much failed in accomplishing that goal in this area.

As a younger man, I was one of eight individuals who had enrolled in a counseling seminar. In the course, we were talking and discussing our way through many varied topics. One particular day, the seminar leader came in and announced, "Today we are going to be discussing sexual issues, and our first topic is masturbation." He turned to me and said, "Frank, what do you think about masturbation?" I immediately wondered why he decided to ask me first. Fortunately, he saw the surprised look on my face and clarified his question with these words, "Is masturbation a sin?"

I quickly responded, "No, it is not sin, but it can be." Immediately, my fellow attendees launched into a verbal barrage, vehemently disagreeing. I took my Bible, held it out, and said, "It's not in here, guys! There are a lot of other sinful things God points out, like a proud look, an arrogant spirit, lying, gossip, envy, jealousy, and selfishness. I don't see masturbation anywhere in here. I believe that if God was all that concerned about the issue of masturbation, He would've put something in His word about it!" Well, the seminar leader went around the room asking each participant their opinion, to which each of the other students responded firmly that masturbation was clearly sinful. The seminar leader then quickly guided the conversation to the next topic. One of the people in the class said, "Wait a minute, sir, what do you think about masturbation? Is it a sin?" At that point he responded, "No, I agree with Frank."

As a class we all wondered. Who was right and who was wrong?

Is masturbation a sin or isn't it? Where should we go for answers? We were all Christians, and we all had the same Bible, but we had all reached very different conclusions. After my experience in that seminar, I was challenged to dig deep into Father's Word and find an answer for myself.

What does the Bible say about masturbation?

I believe digging into Father's Word is the key. It's most important because what the Bible says about an issue should also be what we the church say about that issue. In whatever arena of life where we are pursuing answers, our primary concern must NOT be what others think, or the popular opinion of the day. Our primary concern is always, **what does Father's Word say?**

And here, right at the outset of this discussion, I want to be abundantly clear that my conclusion from my years of study is that Father's Word does not address the issue of masturbation as a sinful behavior.

My friend Scott Brittin, a wonderful pastor and

counselor, affirms that masturbation is not in the Bible. I particularly appreciate his approach to the situation. In a recent conversation, he remarked to me: "When it comes to masturbation, I look at a passage like the one found in Deuteronomy 22:6-7:

> *If you happen to come upon a bird's nest along the way, in any tree or on the ground, with young ones or eggs, and the mother sitting on the young or on the eggs, you shall not take the mother with the young; you shall certainly let the mother go, but the young you may take for yourself, in order that it may be well with you and that you may prolong your days.*

If God was so specific on issues to mention not taking a bird and the eggs or young, why in the world would He not mention masturbation—especially if some of us seem to believe it can cause warts, blindness, and baldness!"

But what about the "sin of Onan?"

Much of the church embraces a common error in their teaching against masturbation. They look at an obscure Old Testament passage buried in Genesis 38 and conclude that God considers the masturbation a sin. They are referring to the sin of Onan.

Now, the first thing one always needs to do when coming to a passage in the Bible is establish the context. Context is the number one rule to follow when interpreting the Bible. I would put it this way: a text, without a context, is a pretext. In other words, if we don't follow the context, we could make the Bible say just about anything we want it to say. We certainly do not want that to happen with this issue of masturbation. Guilt and shame abound in this arena and it is time we arrived at the truth of what this passage is teaching in its context.

In Genesis 38, we are told that Judah had several sons. One of those sons was Er, who had married a woman whose name was Tamar. Er did evil in the sight of the Lord so the Lord took his life, leaving Tamar a childless widow. At this point, Judah instructed his youngest son, named Onan, as per the custom of the day, to provide a child—and more importantly, an heir—for Tamar by having sexual relations with her.

> *And Judah (Onan's father) said to Onan: Go in unto your brother's wife—have sexual relations with her, marry her—and raise up seed to your brother. And Onan knew that the seed would be his (Er's). And it came to pass that when he went into his brother's wife that he spilled it on the ground, lest he should give seed to his brother. And the thing which he did displeased the Lord, therefore the Lord slew him.*

Note that this context is very clear; this passage is, unequivocally, about a man and a woman having sexual relations, NOT about masturbation.

Now, the type of arrangement mentioned in this passage was called "levirate marriage." It was quite common in the ancient world, where most societies were patriarchal. In a patriarchy, an inheritance passes from the father to the children. If a woman in that culture did not have any children, she would not receive an inheritance, and therefore be left destitute. The customs of levirate marriage called for the brother of the man who died to marry his brother's widow and produce an heir with the surviving widow. The child born into the marriage would be considered the child of the dead brother, and that child would receive the inheritance. Out of that wealth, the child would care for its mother. This practice was sanctioned by God in Deuteronomy 25, but that is a whole other issue for another time.

Onan went to his dead brother's wife and refused to bear an heir for her. When they were having sexual relations, he withdrew and spilled his seed on the ground rather than provide an opportunity for her to have a child. This behavior gives us a major glimpse into the character of this man Onan. Notice, he did not mind having sexual relations with his brother's widow, he just did not want to risk her getting pregnant. We are dealing here with a very self-centered, manipulative man. He didn't want to preserve his brother's genealogical line because he didn't want his father's inheritance divided up any further. His selfishness and greed led him to not only disobey his father's expressed wishes but also to callously ignore the needs of his brother's wife. By spilling his seed on the ground, he ensured that his brother's widow would remain childless and be cut out of the inheritance. Some interpreters claim that this passage teaches that it is sinful to "waste seed." This passage in their eyes, mandates that masturbation is sinful because it "wastes seed." The context, however, is very clear. The issue is not wasted seed. The problem was the sinful, selfish, lustful heart of Onan.

Onan spilled his seed because he wanted the entire inheritance for himself. If he produced an heir for his brother, he would lose a portion of the inheritance to his brother's family. If no heir was produced, the inheritance would pass to him. God decided to discipline Onan for his selfishness, greed, and disobedience, and take his life.

Do you see how God's swift punishment of Onan was about his disobedient and abusive heart? Do you see how this passage is not about masturbation at all? It is faulty interpretation to read this passage and conclude that the act of masturbation is sinful. This portion of scripture isn't about masturbation at all! If it was, then we should expect all masturbators to be struck dead. And let's be honest... there wouldn't be many of us left if that were the case.

So since Father's word is truly silent on masturbation, how are we to handle this issue? Simply put, we need to examine the Bible further. In it, we will find definitive principles which address masturbation indirectly.

Father's Word holds the answer.

What I desperately want you to understand is that

our Father's Word is the ultimate authority for governing our lives. We must take great care to make sure we interpret correctly what He affirms—and be careful to not add our opinions and bias to His affirmations.

In 2 Peter 1:2...*"Know this: that no prophecy of the Scripture is of any private interpretation."* Peter is instructing us that we cannot come to the Word of God and just make it say what we want it to say. We do not have the right to do that. We have to let the Bible say what it says without adding to it. This is called interpreting the Bible literally.

"The prophecy came not at any time by the will of man, but holy men of God spoke as they were moved by the Holy Spirit."

This verse teaches us that man did not write this book. God wrote this book! God wrote the Bible. He was very intentional about what went INTO the Bible—and equally intentional about what did NOT go into the Bible.

Finally, this verse also informs us "how" God accomplished the writing of our Bibles. We are told that the Holy Spirit so worked in those men that His presence led them to write what God wanted them to write. Though each author's individual personality is expressed through their writing, each one was able to communicate the truth of God to us concerning the essential things we need to know about life.

Isn't that exciting? We do not have to be in the dark about what is really important in this life—the Bible is a trustworthy guide for us on our journey. God Himself tells us that. We can read it in 2 Timothy 3:16-17, where we are told that *"all scripture is given by inspiration of God, and is profitable for doctrine, for reproof, for correction, for instruction in righteousness: that the man of God may be perfect, thoroughly furnished unto all good works."*

When we have questions about the various issues of life, the first place we need to go is the Word of God. In the Bible, God Himself is instructing, correcting, and teaching us what He says concerning what is right and what is wrong. In other words, the Bible is a one-stop shop for knowing how to live our lives! When we approach Father's Word looking for instruction or teaching on a specific issue, we must ask two questions:

1. Does the Bible address this issue specifically?

2. If not, are there other principles from His Word we can apply to the issue at hand?

In other words, are there other issues that when accompanied with the act of masturbation transform masturbation into a sinful act? For this, we must again go deep into Father's Word.

WHEN DOES MASTURBATION BECOME SINFUL?

So far, we've determined that masturbation in and of itself is not sinful. It's not right or wrong on its own. It's 'amoral'.

So, can masturbation ever be sinful?

The Bible tells us in I Timothy 4 that in all things we are called to moderation. In all things we are to have balance. Eating and drinking becomes a problem when you do either of those things to excess. If you drink too much wine, you will get drunk and being drunk is specifically mentioned in the Bible as a sin. If you eat too much food, that's gluttony—also specifically mentioned in the Bible as being sinful.

An amoral act also becomes sinful when it becomes an end in and of itself. What I mean by that is we see the behavior in question as a source of life for us and it becomes something we cannot live without. Rather than recognizing God as our source of fulfillment, we become preoccupied with the blessing that has been given to us instead of the One Who blessed us and gave us the gift in the first place. When that happens, we have fallen into what the Bible calls idolatry. Idolatry is not an external issue; the problem is not with whatever the idol happens to be. Idolatry occurs when we allow anyone or anything the supreme place in our hearts that only God should have. This can happen to us in so many ways. For example, we can find our fulfillment in our life from such innocent and amoral things as being a soccer player, from performing in our careers, from our spouses, or our families...

We can all turn wonderful things into sinful things— depending on if we let them have too big a place in our hearts. Does that make sense? I hope so because this is what can happen with masturbation. We have already determined that it is an amoral issue, but how we approach it can in fact turn it into a moral issue—a sinful issue!

Masturbation becomes sinful when it is accompanied with lustful thoughts.

Remember the counseling story from earlier, when I shared the question that was asked of me during a counseling seminar? Let's revisit that story and delve further into the conversation. I was sitting in the small circle of counselors, and the professor said, "Frank, is masturbation a sin?" My answer was,

"No, but it can be." At that point, my response was met with general incredulity and skepticism by my fellow classmates. "I don't think it's a sin," I said, "otherwise, God would have said something about it in His Word. However, the Bible does instruct us to not entertain lustful or impure thoughts. If you can masturbate without having sinful thoughts, then masturbation would remain an amoral act and would not in and of itself be sinful." At this point of course, there had to be a smart-aleck who rather sarcastically chimed in, "Well, what do you do then, think about baseball?"

"Yes! If that's what it takes to keep your mind off of something sinful!"

By keeping your mind set on something sinful, you are adding something to the amoral act of masturbation that transforms it into a sinful act. As with many, many other behaviors which are not necessarily sinful on their own, masturbation (or eating, or drinking) becomes sinful because of impure motives or thought patterns. Using pornography for stimulation while masturbating would be an example.

But if we can eat, or drink, or masturbate without sinful thoughts or motives then the amoral behavior remains amoral.

It stands to reason then, masturbation becomes sinful when we dwell on sinful thoughts.

Matthew 5:28 says this: *"to lust in your mind, in the eyes of God is the same as committing adultery."* To even think about adultery is the same as physically committing the act!

This is why Paul tells us to *"bring every thought captive into the obedience of Christ"* (2 Corinthians 10:5). Why? Because sinful thoughts turn amoral behavior into immoral behavior. Sinful thoughts turn normal, natural acts into sin. The issue here is the wrong source: the flesh! When God is left out of the equation you always end up with a sinful result.

Let's clarify this further. Say you're out for a walk, and you come across a guy who's building a house. Is there anything wrong with what he's doing? Obviously not. You strike up a conversation with the builder. It quickly becomes obvious that his life revolves around this house; it drives him! He is absorbed by his house! He is committed to his house. He is self-determined and he is driven. Building the house, a typically normal, even noble activity to partake in, has become sinful. Why? Because for this fellow, building the house has become the controlling, dominant influence in his life. The man has turned an amoral action (building a house) into a sinful one. For him, building the house became sinful the moment he started looking to it, rather than God for his contentment, sense of purpose, or his fulfillment. When you squeeze God out of the moment, then a regular, natural behavior becomes a sinful act. Does that make sense?

In summary, masturbation becomes sinful when you dwell on sinful thoughts.

Masturbation becomes sinful when it interferes with your sexual obligations in marriage.

Let's visit 1 Corinthians 7:2. Paul says, *"To avoid for-nication, let every man have his own wife and let every woman have her own husband."*

This verse unequivocally affirms that all of us, men and women, have a sexual identity and desire. It also affirms that sexual sin is NOT primarily a male issue. Paul addresses both men AND women. Masturba-tion isn't only a guy thing. Paul continues:

> *Let the husband therefore render unto the wife her due, and likewise also the wife to the hus-band. The wife has not power of her own body, but the husband. And likewise the husband does not have power of his own body, but the wife. Defraud you not, one the other except to be with consent for a time you may give your-selves to fasting and prayer.*

When we get married, the Bible teaches us that we become one. At this point, though remaining indi-viduals, we no longer have the authority over our individual bodies. Our bodies actually belong to our spouse. If you as a marriage partner are masturbat-ing as a replacement, or to avoid having to go to your spouse for sexual union, then masturbation becomes sinful. Most times, this sort of sinful masturbation is done in secrecy. It occurs without the other spouse knowing.

Ephesians 5 has some great words about doing things in secret. Check out verse 8:

> *You were once darkness, but now you are light in the Lord. Therefore what? Walk as children of light, for the fruit of the spirit in all goodness and righteousness and truth proving what acceptable unto the Lord, and have no fellowship with the unfruitful works of darkness, but rather reprove them for it is a shame to even speak of those things which are done of them in secret.*

As Christians, we are not to walk in secrecy. Whenever I hear of someone doing something in secret, my yellow flags start going up! Whatever we are doing, we ought to be able to do without secrecy. Masturbation, pursued without the other partner's knowledge and consent would make the masturbation event a sinful one.

It's not uncommon for work demands to necessitate spouses spending lengthy amounts of time apart. We need to be honest here and affirm that the sex drive does not go into neutral during these lengthy separations and is going to continue to scream quite loudly. Masturbation can be an important tool in such a circumstance—one we'll discuss more a bit later on.

Masturbation becomes sinful when it has mastery over you.

Does the urge to masturbate control you? Has

masturbation become habitual? Something you now HAVE to do? If so, this amoral behavior has become sinful for you. Scripture addresses this issue very clearly in Romans 6:11-16: *"Whatever you yield yourself to becomes your master."* And then in Matthew 6:24: *"No one can serve two masters."*

Is masturbation controlling you, or are you in control of your masturbation? Paul said in 1 Corinthians 9:27, *"I buffet my body to bring it into submission."* He's saying, I'm going to have the mastery over my body. My body is not going to have mastery over me.

Ephesians 5:18 sums up our directive from God: we are to be *filled* with the Holy Spirit. The Greek word used for 'fill' is the word *plereo*, and it means "controlled". My body doesn't control me—the Holy Spirit controls me. As believers, we don't yield control of our lives to anyone or anything other than the Holy Spirit and the revealed Word of God. Does that make sense?

The danger here, my friends, is that masturbation can control us. It can become habitual. It can become an obsession and can lead us deep into other sins—like pornography. Pornography is an incredibly dangerous trap, similar to drug usage. When it is used for stimulation, it requires higher and higher 'doses' which in turn deepens the addiction. My friend, we are to have only one master and that is the God who loves us and has our very best interests at heart.

Masturbation becomes sinful when it leads to self-indulgence.

The dictionary defines self-indulgence as pleasing yourself or doing exactly what you feel like doing—especially as it pertains to pleasure or idleness. Self-indulgence is immersing yourself in pleasurable activities simply for the purpose of making yourself feel better, pampering yourself, etc. At its core, it is selfish, self-centered behavior and it's a lifestyle that God stands against. The Christian life is meant to be others-centered, and self-indulgence runs in direct opposition to God's design.

Please understand, I am NOT saying it is sinful to enjoy life and enjoy the things God has created for us. I Timothy 6 teaches that God has given us richly all things. In Philippians 2, Paul makes it very clear that there is nothing wrong with looking out for our own interests. The issue is that we are not to be consumed with our interests to the neglect of serving the interests of others as well. It is very easy for us as fleshly beings to be consumed with meeting our own fleshly needs, and this attitude can transform any amoral behavior into a sinful one. Even perfectly acceptable recreational activities or hobbies can slide into self-indulgence.

Take soccer for example. If you're playing soccer for *you*, in order to get a sense of "life" out of it, soccer becomes idolatry. In that moment you are looking to something other than God as your source of life. Be very careful of things or activities that focus on yourself; be careful that they don't become so self-indulgent and self-gratifiying that those things replace God and His will for our lives that we love others. It is very easy to be consumed with your own well-being and forget about the well-being of your teammates. Do you remember Paul's instructions in 1 Corinthians 7? Did he say "to avoid fornication, let each man masturbate, let each wife masturbate?" No. *"To avoid fornication, let each man have his own wife, and let each wife have her own husband."* Paul made it very clear that Father's answer to the sex drive was not masturbation, but marriage. God designed and sanctioned marriage and the sexual union in marriage as the norm for all men and all women. The only real exception as later detailed in I Corinthians 7 was the gift of singleness.

The point I would make here is that masturbation is a sexual outlet only until marriage. It was never intended by God to become such an issue of self-orientation that a person fails to seek a spouse. I have met such people in the counseling arena. Essentially they had become compulsively "married" to their own body. Scripture is clear: if you don't have that gift of singleness, you should be pursuing a spouse.

Summary

As we have seen, the Bible is our trustworthy guide for determining whether or not a behavior is sinful. We have also seen that the Bible does NOT address the issue of masturbation directly, leaving us to conclude the masturbation event in itself is not sinful.

And we have looked at principles from God's Word which, when violated, make the masturbation event a sinful one.

Masturbation is sinful when:

- you think impure thoughts
- you neglect your sexual obligations in marriage
- you allow it to have mastery over you
- it becomes self-indulgent

Now, does Father's Word give us any principles to help keep masturbation from becoming sinful?

KEEPING MASTURBATION SINLESS

We have already confirmed that amoral behaviors become sinful when they are linked with sinful thoughts or motives.

Here's a glorious, provocative thought for you. If sinful practices make amoral behavior sinful, could sanctified principles make an amoral behavior righteous? ABSOLUTELY! The Bible heralds this reality to us loud and clear.

First, in I Timothy 4:4-5 the Bible tells us that we are to *"receive what God has created, and sanctify it through the Word and prayer with thanksgiving."* When we do this, we fulfill the charge in I Corinthians 9 that whatever we do, even when it comes to such mundane things as eating and drinking, we do so to the glory of God!

Do you realize what this is saying? We can work to the glory of God. We can drive our car to the glory

of God. We can change diapers to the glory of God.
By maintaining a spirit of thanksgiving and prayer
to God we can actually transform any and all of our
behaviors (except clearly revealed sinful ones) into
acts of worship. If the truth be told, there are only
two kinds of behavior—glorious ones and inglori-
ous ones, sinful behaviors and sanctified behaviors.
When I am abiding in Christ even brushing my teeth
becomes a glorious act of worship to God.

Bring God into the equation.

It is my conviction that masturbation is not only kept
from being sinful when one's thoughts are kept pure,
but that masturbation can be transformed through
praise and thanksgiving into a spiritual act before
God.

Please allow me to explain. The Apostle Paul gives
us clear directions for maintaining a pure thought
life in 1 Corinthians 10:5 and Colossians 3:17. First,
he writes *"bring every thought captive into the obedience of Christ."* Compare each thought that enters
your mind with the truth of Christ. Second, in terms
of behavior, *"Whatever you do, in word or deed do
it all in the name of the Lord Jesus Christ, giving
thanks to God."* The Bible makes it clear that we are
to ensure that our words and actions are coming
from a place of obedience and thankfulness to God.

According to Paul, our words and actions are either
saintly, or they're not. There's no middle ground.
The sole alternative to saintly behavior is sinful

behavior. There is no in-between state. You're either being sinful and carnal, or you're being saintly and spiritual. You're either abiding in Christ or you're not abiding in Christ. Bottom line. Simple as that.

Abiding in Christ means that through our faith in Jesus, God now lives in us, and we live in Him as our life source. I believe that abiding in Christ is in fact our default mode as believers. We are abiding in Him, drawing life from Him, until we make the choice to derive life from a source other than Him. Let's say that you've got a radio sitting on your desk. It was designed to be plugged into an outlet. As long as it's plugged in, it can function the way it was designed to function. My friends, that is a picture of our own abiding in Christ, and it is this abiding in Him that transforms all of our behavior into that which honors and glorifies God.

Before we were in Christ, we were in Adam, disconnected from God. Throughout our lives, we made our abode in sin. All we did was sin, because we had the wrong source. The moment we accepted the Lord Jesus Christ, the Holy Spirit reconnected us to God through the person and work of the Lord Jesus Christ. We now abide in Him, and He in us, and this will always be true for us. This is the glory of the New Covenant that Jesus established. We have been restored to God permanently. Now, in our day to day living, this is the norm for our lives. We live out of the God Who lives in us. Throughout the New Testament however, we are told that we can make moment by moment choices to try and find life from sources other than God. Allow me to illustrate again with that radio on the desk.

Your radio is sitting on your desk, plugged into the wall and playing well in its default mode. However, if you look on the back of most radios, you'll find a little switch. Flick that switch and you're now on battery power. Though connected to the wall as its default, the radio has now switched to drawing its power from another source. My friend, that is exactly how it is for us. We have a choice. At any moment we can make the choice to function on battery power, on our own resources, instead of Christ's resources. This is what transforms our behavior, even our good behavior, into sinful behavior. It's all about the source.

When a person masturbates while setting their mind on God while thanking Him and praising Him for creating them a sexual being, masturbation becomes more than 'not sinful.' Masturbation, bathed in pure thoughts and accompanied by prayer, is an act of worship to the God who made us sexual beings.

Recently, a young man came into my office and told me he was struggling with masturbation. He told me he was wrestling with guilt and impure thoughts. "Good for you," I said, "I'm glad you're struggling. You *ought* to be struggling because your mind is in the wrong place! Here's what you are going to do moving forward. Colossians 3 tells us to set our mind on things above, so you are going to stop thinking sinful thoughts when you are masturbating and replace them with Biblical thoughts."

Incidentally, the phrase "set your mind" is in the

imperative mood... meaning it is a command. If the Holy Spirit through Father's Word commands us to set our minds, what does that tell us? It tells us we *can* set our minds! It tells us that as we abide in Christ, you and I will have the ability to set our minds in the place where they need to be.

I told this young man that from now on, he was to set aside the sinful thoughts and pornographic images. Instead, he was to set his mind on the Lord Jesus Christ and prayerfully fulfil the act of masturbation with thanksgiving and praise. Something like this:

Father, thank you that you have made my body to work like this. Thank you that this is exciting. Thank you that this feels good. Thank you that I can do this. Thank you that I can have this release. Father, I look forward to the day when I'm going to be married, but until I'm married I have this outlet for which I praise you and thank you!

I believe with all my heart that this simple idea transforms masturbation, an amoral and potentially sinful act, into an act of worship! When the single person celebrates their sexuality along with the God who created them as sexual beings, this will provide a Biblically legitimate alternative to the sinful choices of adultery and promiscuity. Further, the shame, the guilt, the obsessive thoughts, the pornography—will be gone! They will be replaced with thoughts of praise to God, love for who He is to us. We genuinely thank Him for making us sexual beings, instead of allowing our God-given sexuality to be turned into something sinful.

My friend, as I have shared these principles over the years, countless people have come back to me and reported that they have indeed been able to set their minds and enter into freedom. I'm always overjoyed, time and again, to hear how they experience control over their masturbation instead of their masturbation having control over them. Put simply, they are entering into the freedom that Jesus died to bring them.

So often, I hear the all too simplistic response: masturbation is a sin! Don't do it! Interestingly enough, it's almost always married people saying those things to single people. It's easy for someone with a sexual drive who has the outlet of marriage to say that. Is it fair, or is it even love, to say that to single people who do not have the outlet of marriage for their sexual drive? Don't do that to them! Instead lead them to the face of God where they can pursue this thing Biblically and honestly and with praise and thanksgiving to the God who has made them sexual beings. Does that make sense?

Don't keep masturbation secret!

We've already established that when a spouse uses masturbation to withhold sexual union from their spouse, then masturbation becomes sinful. Additionally, if masturbation is kept secret, it becomes sinful.

Shedding light on masturbation is the single most important thing you can do to keep it from becoming sinful. Address it with your spouse. As with all things pertaining to marriage, communication here is crucial.

It's not uncommon for spouses to spend lengthy time apart from each other, often due to work demands. After a child is born, the wife will need to abstain from sexual union for at least a period of six weeks, and what about professional athletes who often have to be away from home for extended periods of time? We need to be honest here and affirm that the sex drive does not go into neutral during these lengthy separations; in fact, it will begin screaming loudly. When agreed upon by both parties, masturbation is a way for married couples to alleviate that tension and help defend against the possibility for immoral behavior. It would be well within Biblical boundaries to share sweet thoughts together over the phone and enjoy a semblance of intimacy through modern technology. I am being very serious here. I have shared this and had couples very much enjoy each other with miles of distance between them, as they looked forward to wonderful reunions face to face.

If you are masturbating at home, you need to communicate with your spouse about it. Perhaps they'd like to participate in a mutual way and make it a partnered event. Maybe they'd like to just cuddle or hug together and express love in that way. Incidentally, guys this could be a great solution while your wife is on her period!

Within marriage, masturbation is a helpful release in certain situations, and a safeguard against immorality, but only when it is communicated openly and agreed upon. Keep it in the open. Avoid immorality in your thought life, and maintain sexual union with your spouse.

Keep masturbation from becoming sinful by strictly controlling it.

As funny or odd as this may come across, please know that I'm being very serious with you. Do not have unscheduled, impromptu masturbation. In other words, schedule it. Put it in your daytimer if you have to.

I can just hear someone saying, "Pastor Frank, what do you mean?" I mean exactly what I'm saying. By scheduling masturbation you're able to say "I have control over this thing. It doesn't control me. I dictate when it happens, not my urges." When I do that I am fulfilling the charge Paul brought in I Corinthians 9 to *"buffet my body bringing it into submission."*

This is the fruit of the Spirit called self-control, and we should seek self-control for masturbation and other areas of life as well. There are times, for example, when I want ice cream. Sometimes I want it so bad, that I can taste the ice cream. Now please hear me: there is nothing wrong with ice cream. I am free to have the ice cream. But sometimes I say, "No, I'm not going to, even though I want to."

Why would I do that? Because I want to practice the

Spirit-empowered ability to say no. I want to check myself and see if I have control over the ice cream or the ice cream has control over me.

It's the same with masturbation. My body is to be in submission to me. I have authority over my body. I have control over it; so no impromptu masturbation.

Summary

So let's go over this again, just to be clear. To keep masturbation from becoming sinful we should:

- Bring God into the equation (keep your thoughts pure in an attitude of praise and thanksgiving to God)
- Keep it in the open (no secrets, especially from our spouses)
- Schedule it (don't let it control us)

My friends, as I have taught these Biblical principles, I have seen men and women gain a mastery over masturbation instead of it having mastery over them. I've seen people have the frequency of their masturbation decreased. I've seen them walk free of guilt and shame. I've seen them walk in praise and thanksgiving.

My conviction is that all this occurs because the truth has set them free, just as the Lord Jesus Christ promised it would. Instead of relying on hearsay and the opinion of man, they are appropriating the truth of God's Word to their lives in a complete and dynamic way.

CONCLUSION

As we wind this discussion down, I want to share with you a quote. This comes from an article titled *"Is Masturbation a Sin"* in the November/December 2001 issue of YouthWorker magazine. A youth pastor by the name of Dale Kaufman wrote this. Note that I've changed a few of the words to widen its application.

> *How much false guilt could we alleviate? How many dangerous sexual encounters would be forgone if we were simply open and honest with people about how best to handle their sexuality. We must give them straightforward options and solutions to deal with their bodies. It's imperative that we let them know that masturbation can and should be used as a viable God-honoring way to deal with the stresses of sexuality. With a sex-saturated society all around us, we as pastors, youth pastors, caring adults, need to give men and women the ability to live Godly lives in the midst of a*

perverse culture. Masturbation within Biblical boundaries will give them that ability. It's time to stop standing on the side-lines, hoping that somehow people will get the right information and act on it in the right way. We must become proactive—getting over our own fears and our uncomfortableness, and initiate discussions with people. We must do what is our God-given responsibility as Christians to do. We must help others navigate the stormy waters of their sexuality. May God help us to accomplish that with His Word and under the leading of the Holy Spirit.

So be it.

Dale Kaufman has courageously stepped forward to herald truth and love. He addresses masturbation with a heart for all to hear what the Bible really says about this issue. I believe he treats this issue well and I hope to meet him some day. Let's pray.

Father, I pray that there hasn't been any error in this discussion we've had here, and if there has been, I ask you snatch it away from the hearts of each reader.

But Father, where there has been truth, protect it— even if it's truth that's foreign to us; things we've never heard before. Father, if these things are true, not only protect these things in the hearts and minds of these dear readers, but knit them there, cement them there.

Give us a confidence to go out in the church and community around and provide these principles from Your Word to lead people into freedom. The time for the enemy having his way with guilt and shame and perversity and lust needs to be over, Father. May we all be the warriors you created us to be, handling the sword of truth with tenacity, courage, and love.

And that's going to be my prayer—that we would no longer walk in fear but embrace the mandate to love enough to speak the truth without thinking of our reputation.

So be it, Father. In Jesus' name, amen and amen.

ACKNOWLEDGEMENTS

I owe a great deal of gratitude to my associate in ministry, Tim Chalas. For many years he functioned as the youth pastor at Grace Life Fellowship working with teens. Together we sought with all our hearts to avoid the simplistic cliché and rules-based approach to Christianity that is so often offered to teens. In doing so, this topic came up often and he was an invaluable friend, fellow student, and teacher for me as I worked my way through the Scriptures in an effort to arrive at a Biblical understanding of this issue. He continues to this day in his new role as Executive Pastor at Grace Life Fellowship to encourage and challenge me to seek the truth that sets men free.

LIVING IN GRACE

Living in Grace is the Bible teaching ministry of Frank Friedmann. It exists to help men and women from all walks of life experience and express Jesus. Most Christians live with constant guilt, shame, anxiety, emptiness, and loss. Jesus Christ promises joy, rest, peace, freedom, and abundant life to ALL those who put their faith in Him.

Frank has written several books on living in grace. They're scheduled for release in 2016.

WHERE TO FIND US

Grace Life Fellowship
10210 Baringer Foreman Rd.
Baton Rouge, LA 70809

225-769-8844

For free sermons, articles, videos, and more visit

FrankFriedmann.com

BOOKS BY FRANK FRIEDMANN

The Impossible Christian Life

The Impossible Christian Life Self-Study

Parenting in Grace

Divorce: Could We Have Misunderstood What Jesus Said?

Sex: What Every Teen Should Know

CHILDREN'S BOOKS BY FRANK FRIEDMANN

Who Am I?

I Was Wrong, But God Made Me Right

If I'm Right, Why Do I Keep Doing Wrong?

Made in the USA
Thornton, CO
04/07/23 14:59:25

0680ed1a-af1e-445a-8c54-608576290498R02